mel bay presents

J. S. Bach
for Mandolin

Online Audio

by Robert Bancalari

To Access the Online Audio Go To:
www.melbay.com/95770BCDEB

13 Solos from the book have been recorded on the enclosed CD.

D1609544

1 2 3 4 5 6 7 8 9 0

Visit us on the Web at www.melbay.com — E-mail us at email@melbay.com

Bourrée Angloise

(from Partita in A minor for solo flute)

Johann Sebastian Bach
(1685 - 1750)

4

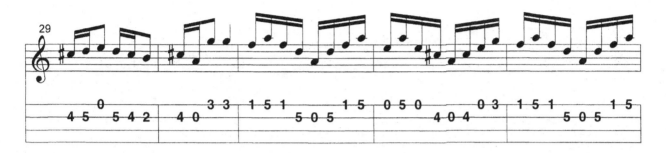

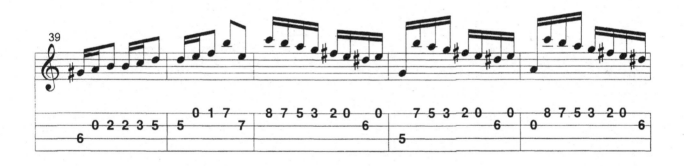

Marche

(from the Anna Magdalena Bach Book)

Johann Sebastian Bach
(1685 - 1750)

Allegro

7

Fantaisie
(from Partita No. III in A minor)

Johann Sebastian Bach
(1685 - 1750)

Allegro Moderato

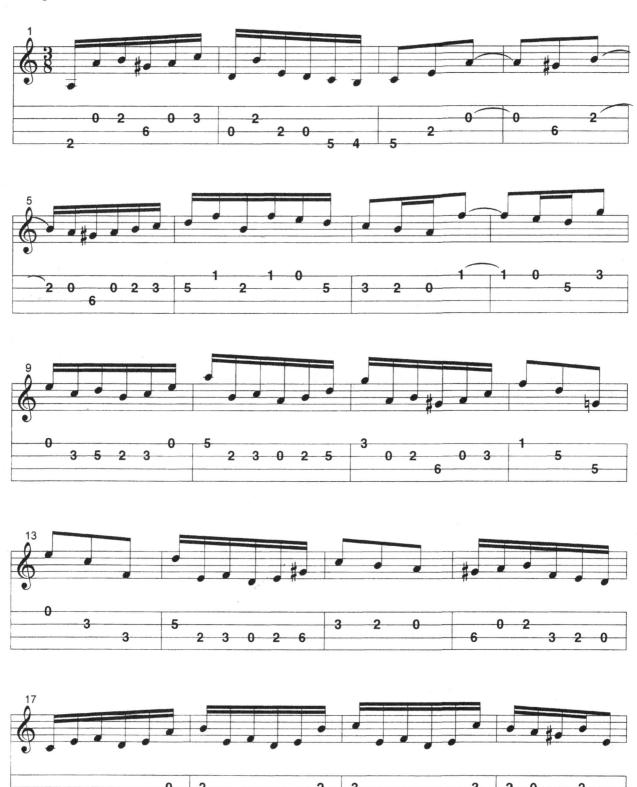

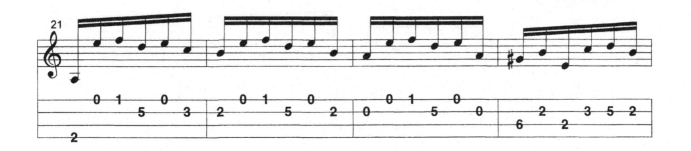

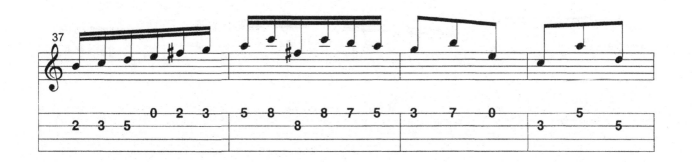

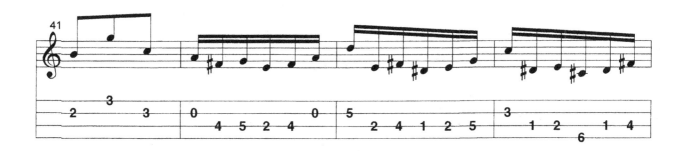

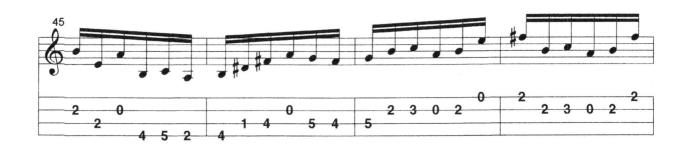

10

11

Marche

(from the Anna Magdalena Bach Book)

Johann Sebastian Bach
(1685 - 1750)

Allegro ma non troppo

14

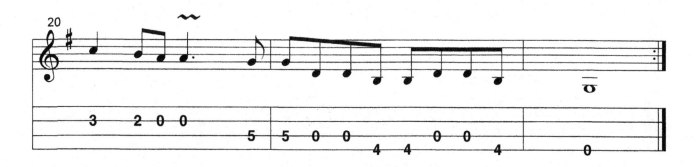

Courante

(from English Suite No. IV in F)

Johann Sebastian Bach
(1685 - 1750)

Passepied I (en Rondeau)
(from English Suite No. V in E minor)

Johann Sebastian Bach
(1685 - 1750)

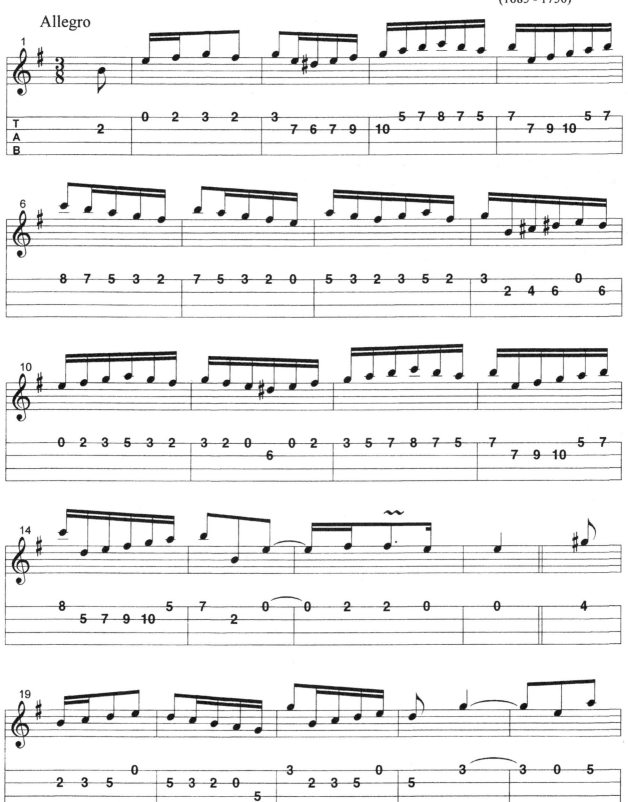

Air
(from French Suite No. IV in Eb)

Johann Sebastian Bach
(1685 - 1750)

Moderato

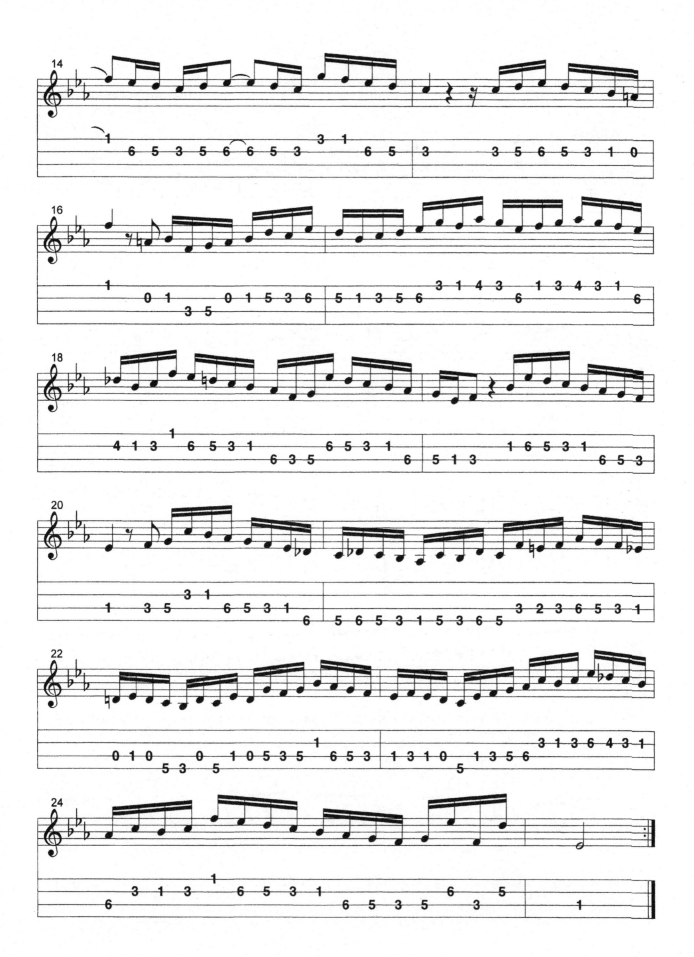

Gavotte I

(from English Suite No. III in G Minor)

Johann Sebastian Bach
(1685 - 1750)

Gavotta

(from Partita No. VI in E minor)

Johann Sebastian Bach
(1685 - 1750)

Un Poco Allegro

Gigue

(from French Suite No. VI in E)

Johann Sebastian Bach
(1685 - 1750)

28

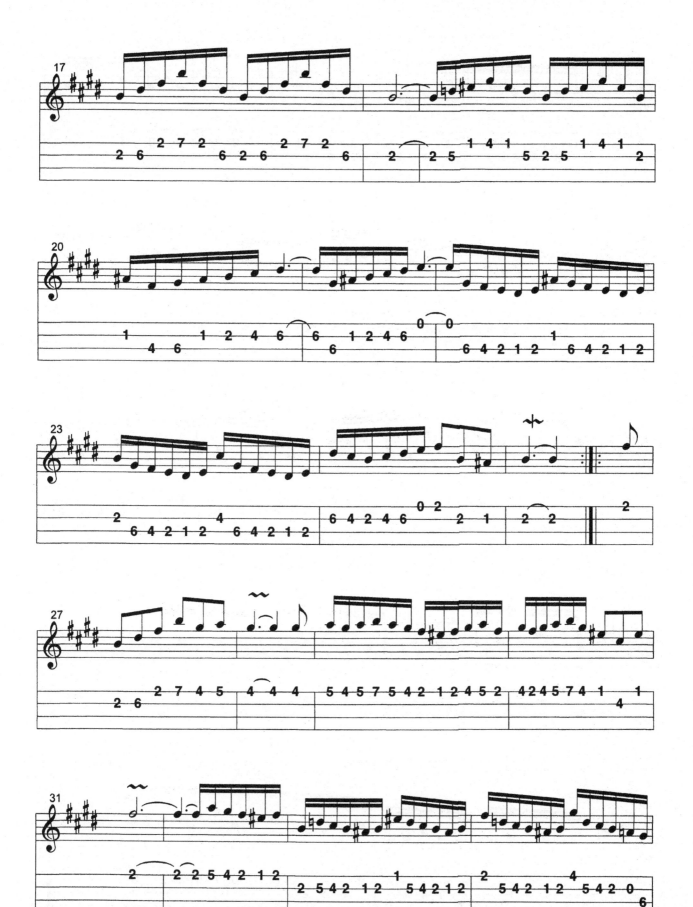

Suite III

(from solo Suites for Cello)

Prelude

Johann Sebastian Bach
(1685 - 1750)

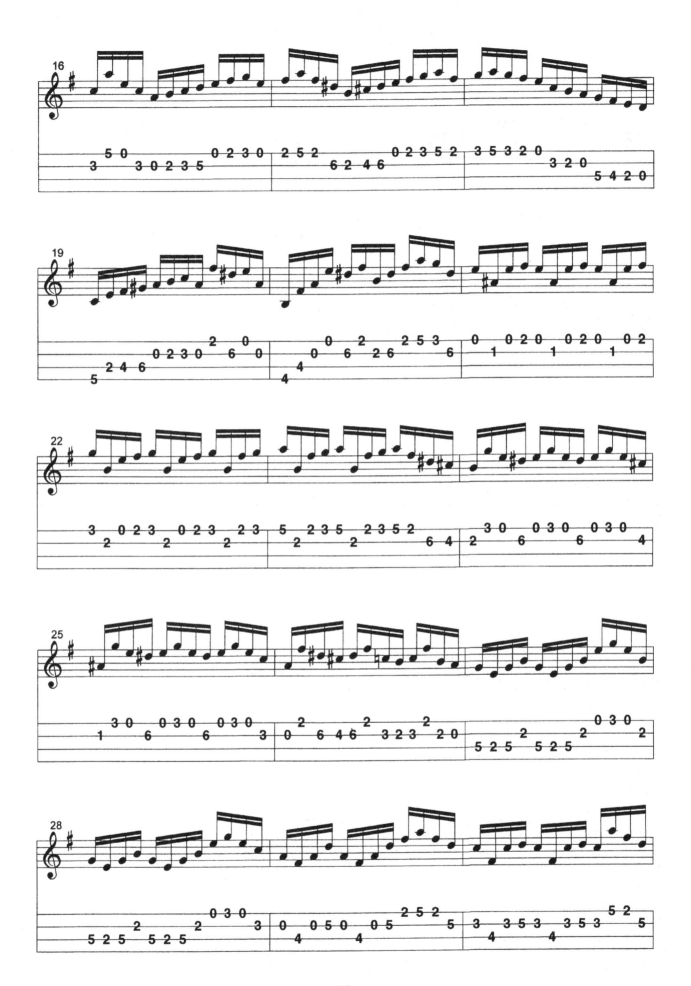

32

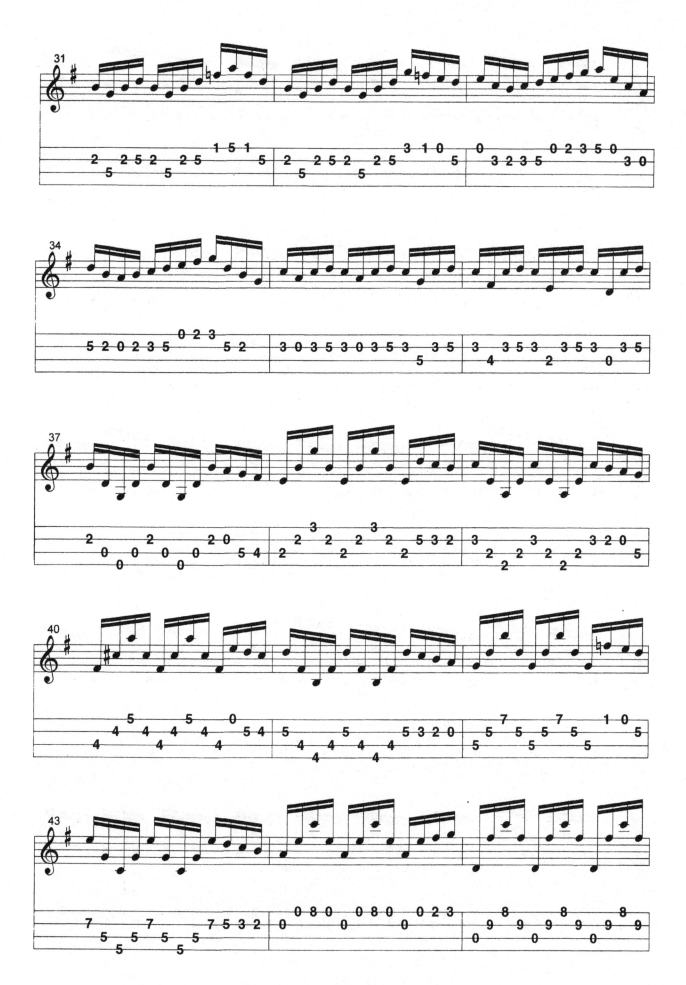

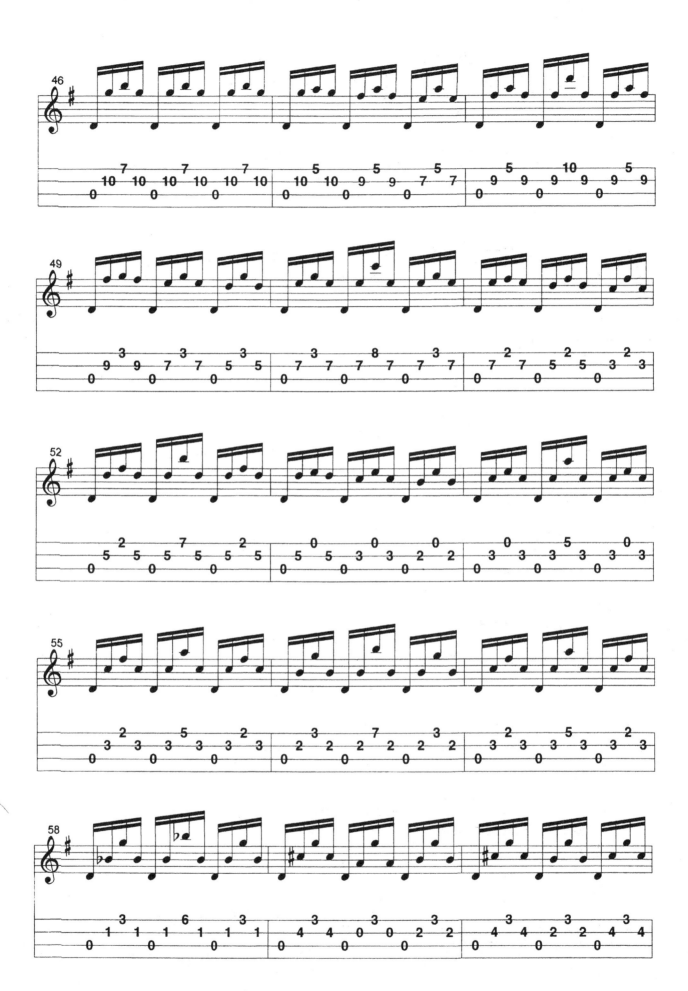

34

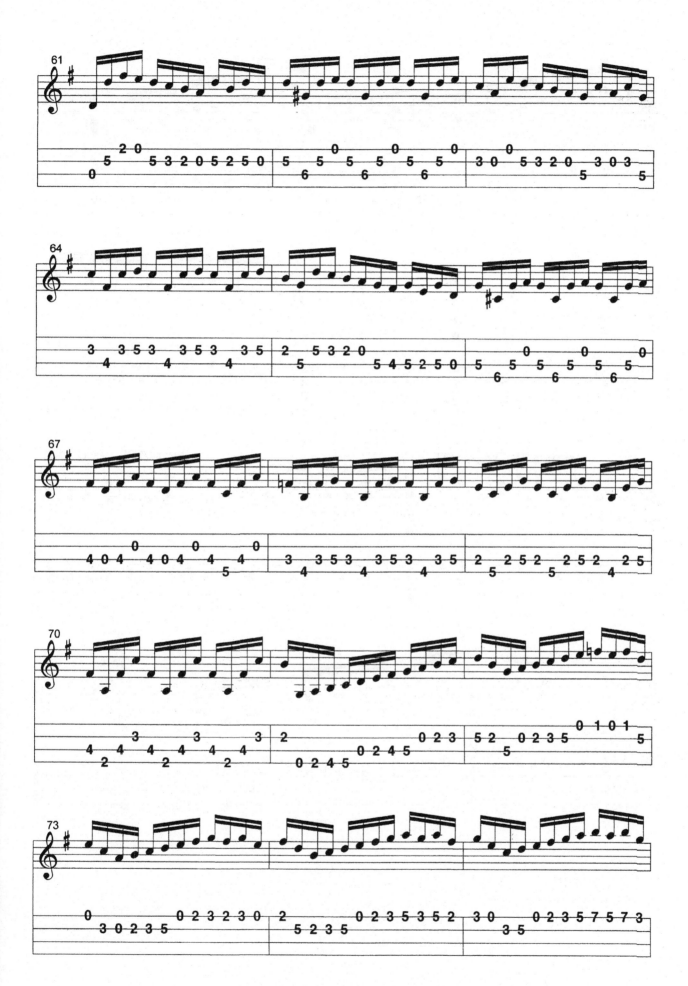

Allemande

Johann Sebastian Bach
(1685 - 1750)

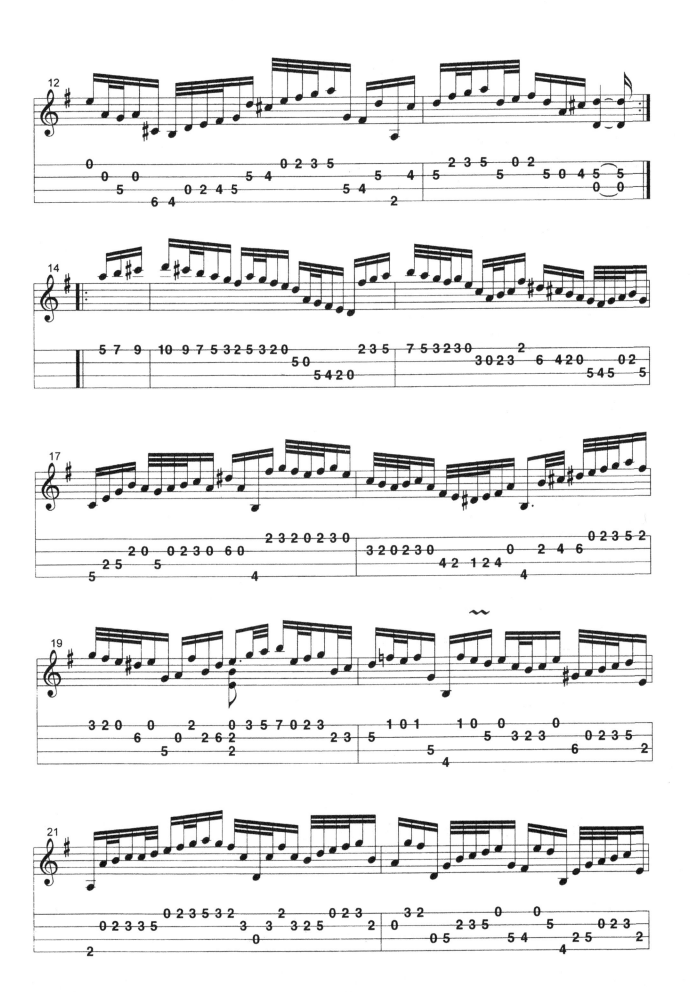

Courante

Johann Sebastian Bach
(1685 - 1750)

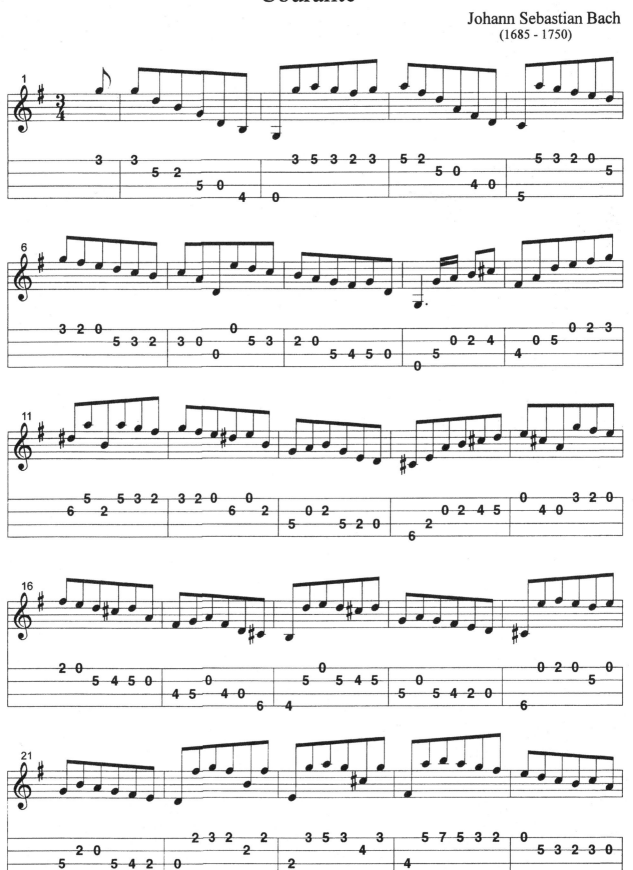

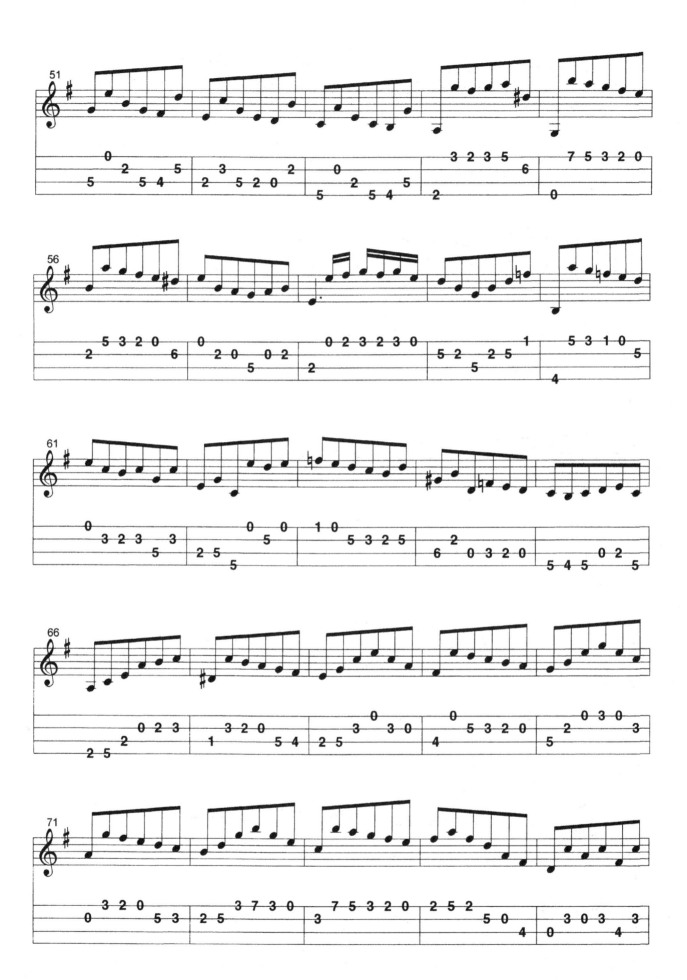

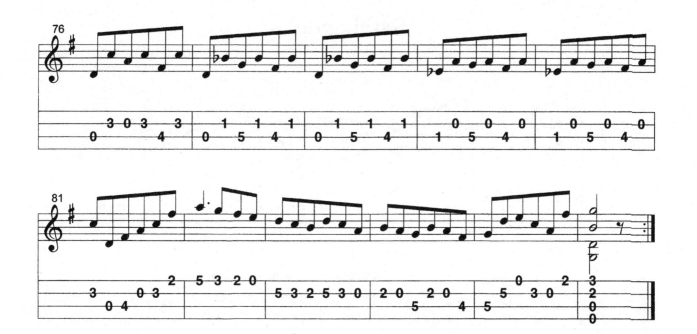

Sarabande

Johann Sebastian Bach
(1685 - 1750)

Bouree I

Johann Sebastian Bach
(1685 - 1750)

Bouree II

Johann Sebastian Bach
(1685 - 1750)

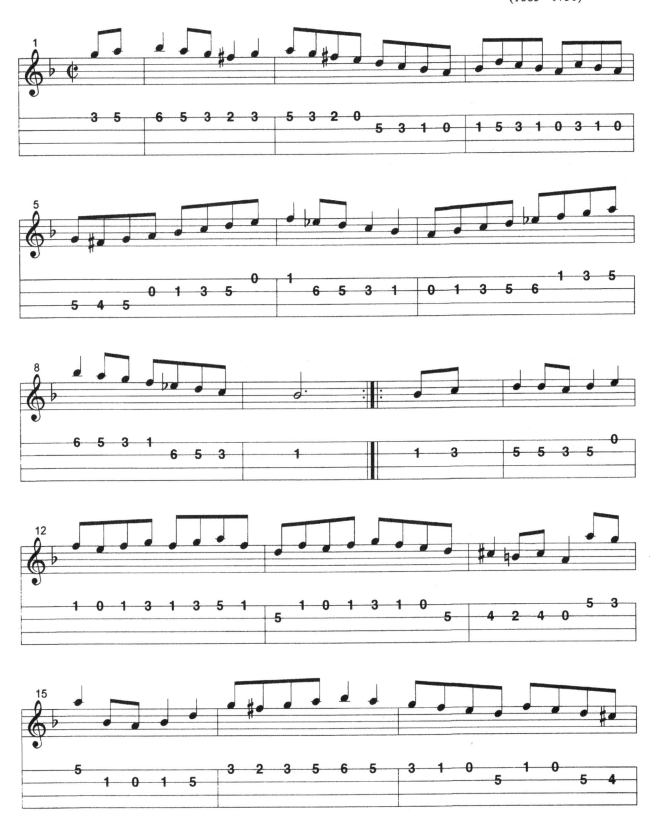

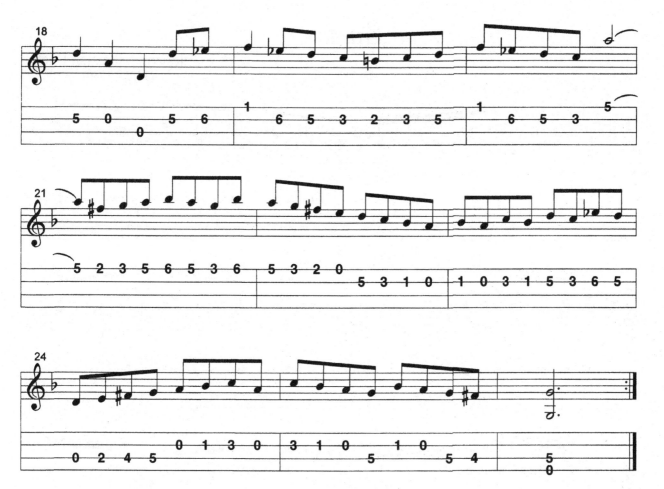

Bouree I D.C.

Gigue

Johann Sebastian Bach
(1685 - 1750)

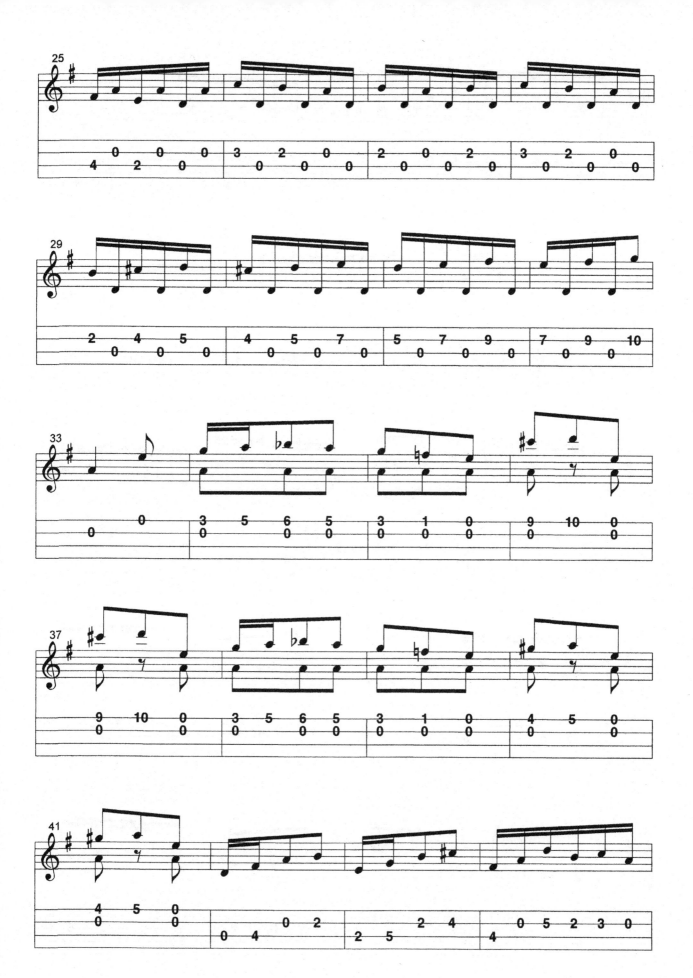

51

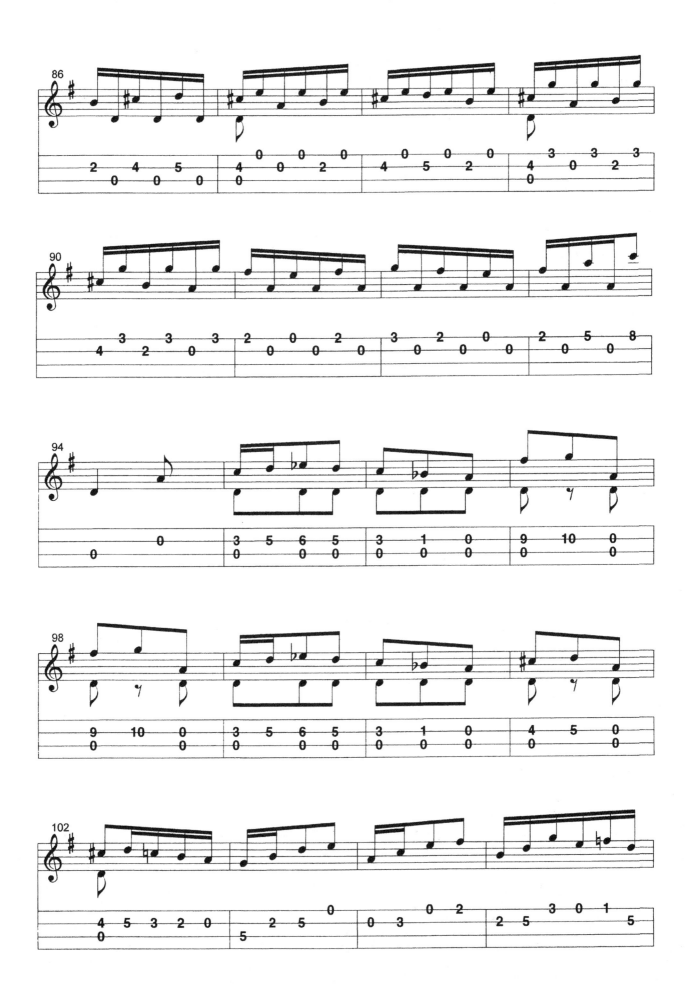

Ciaccona
(from Sonata No. 4 in D minor for solo violin)

Johann Sebastian Bach
(1685 - 1750)

56

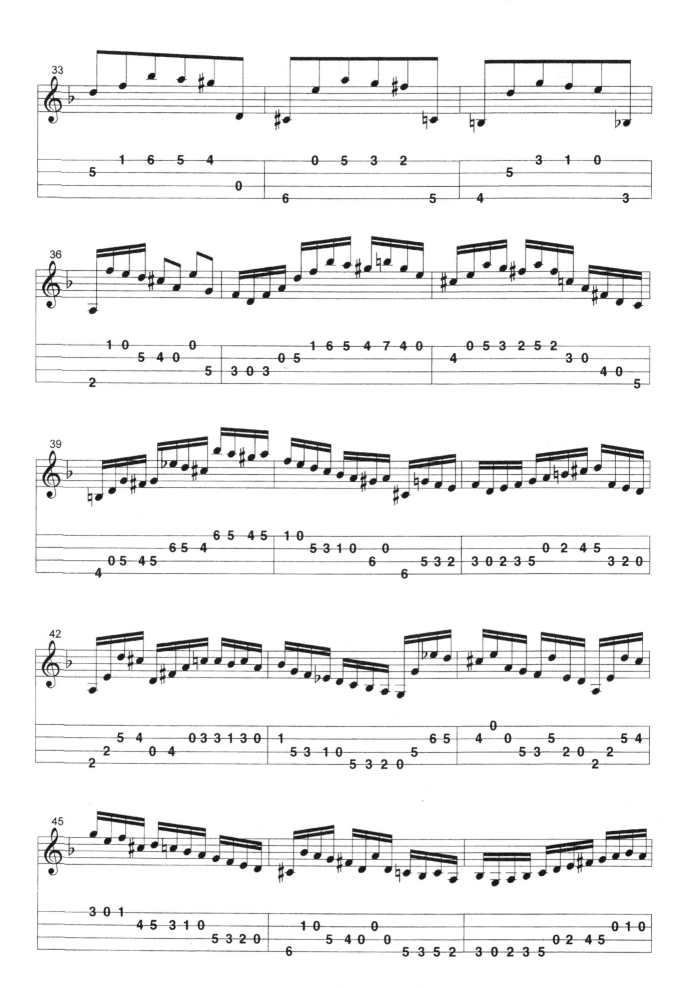

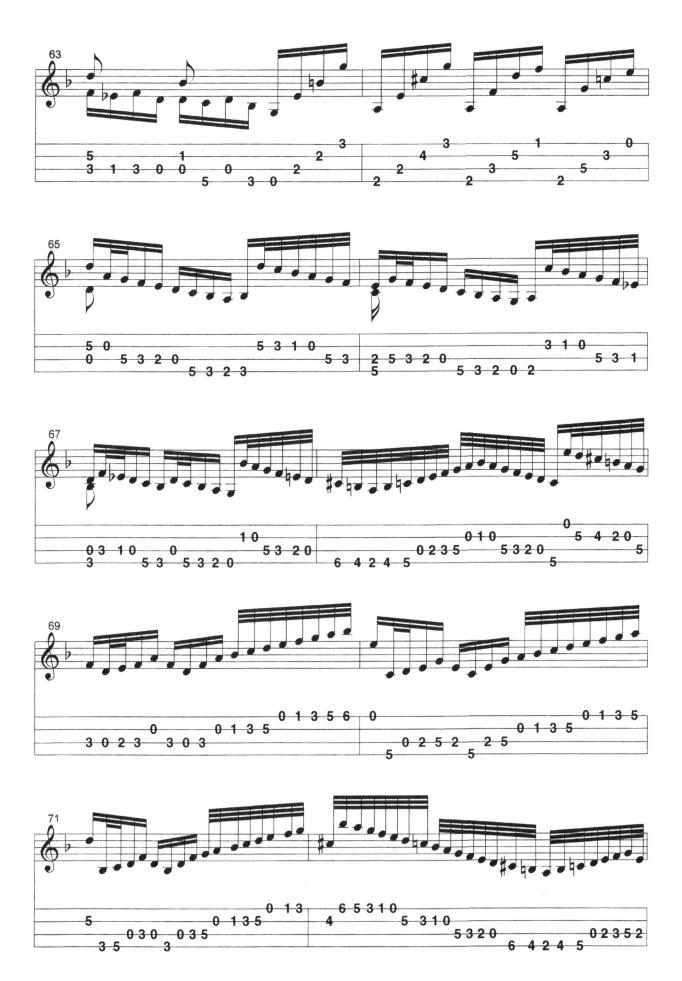

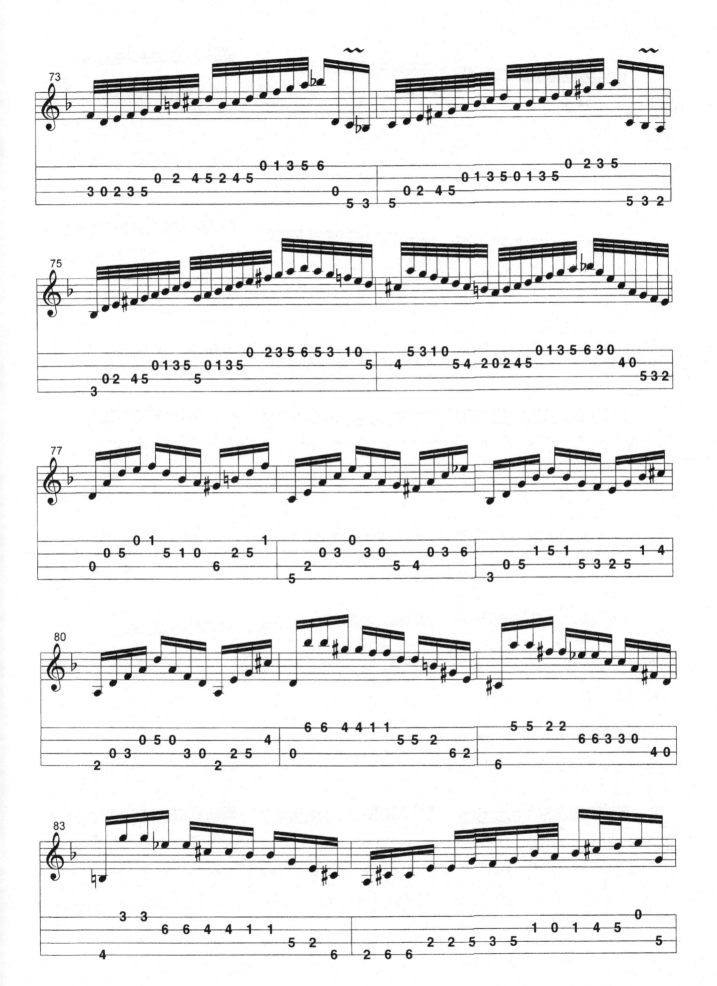

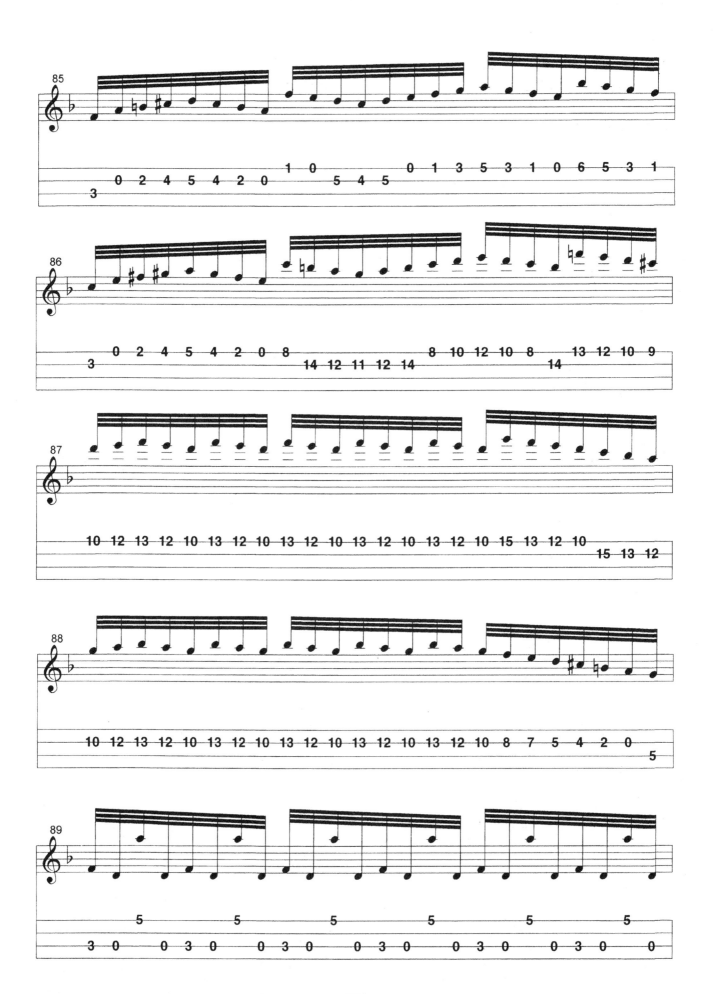

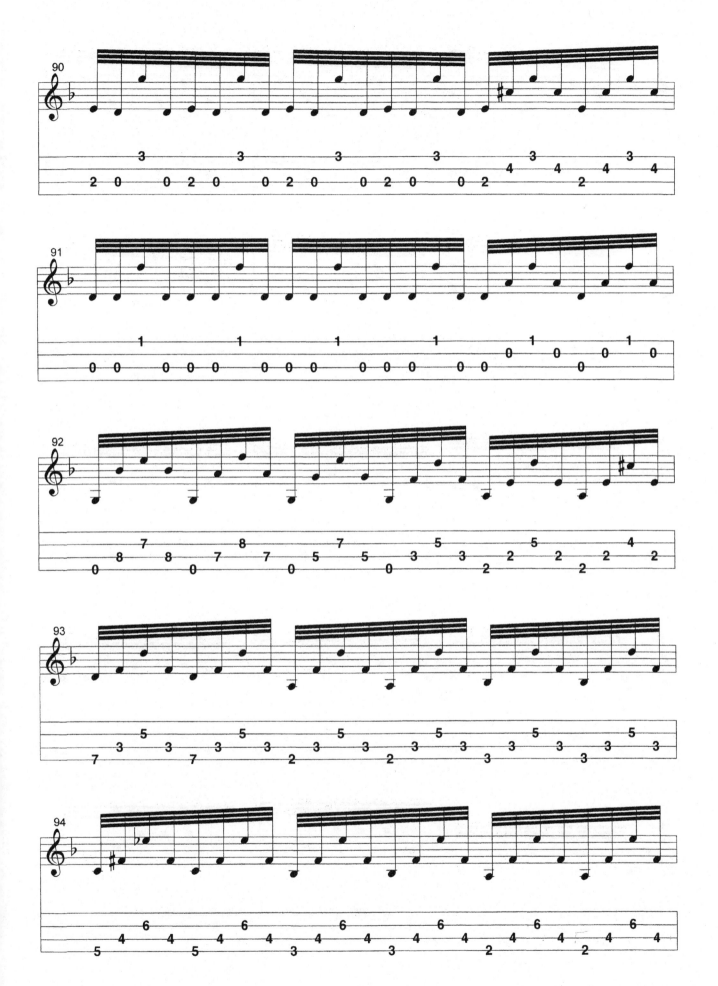

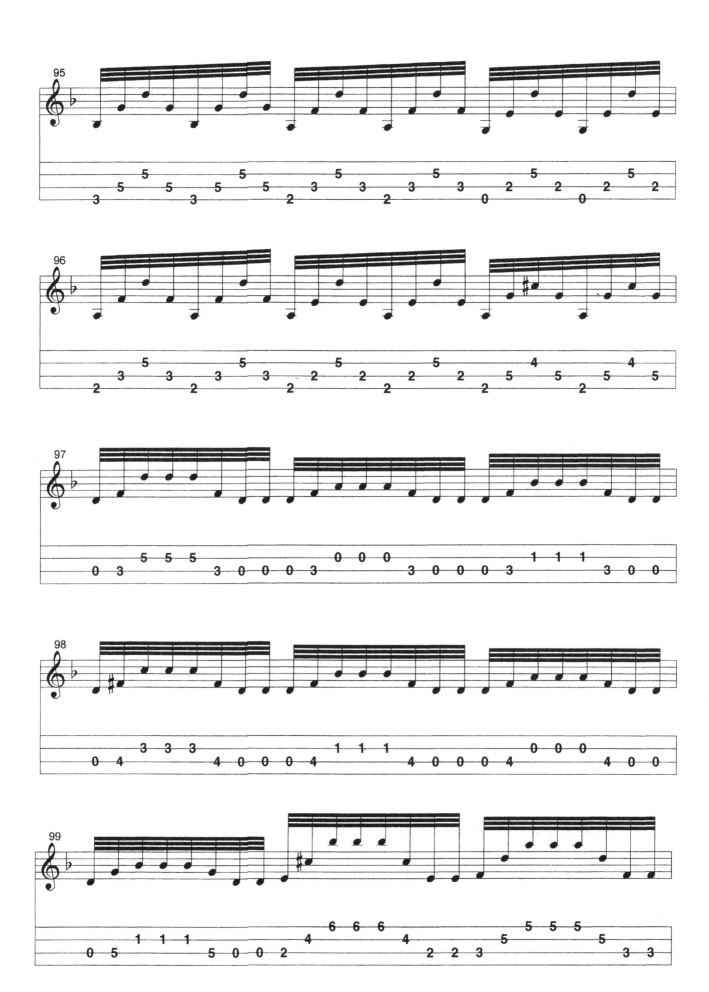

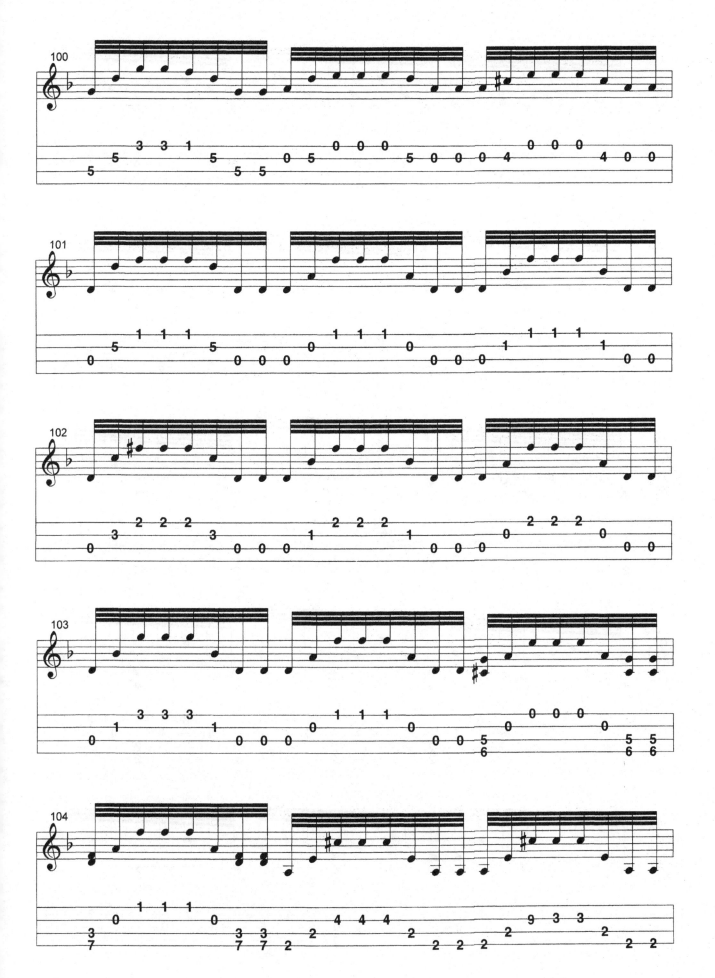

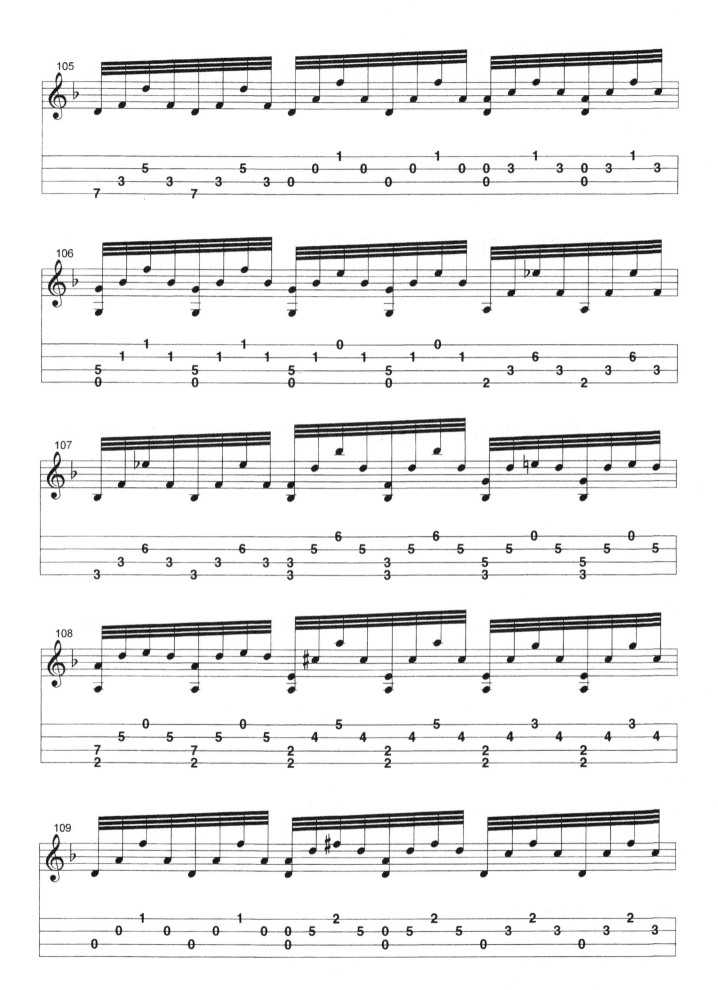

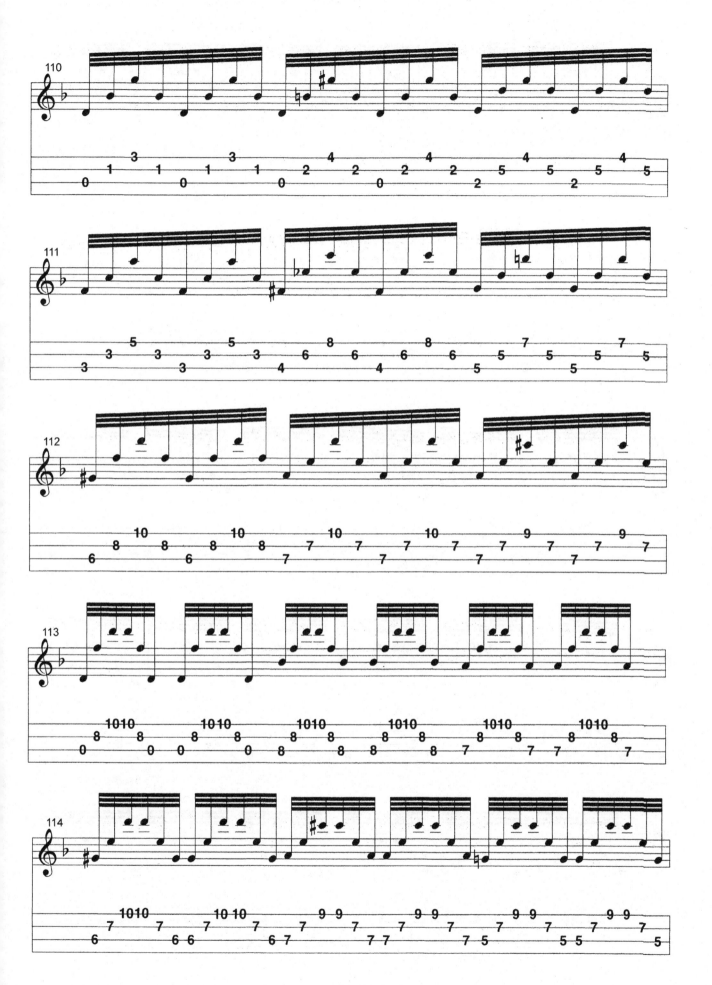

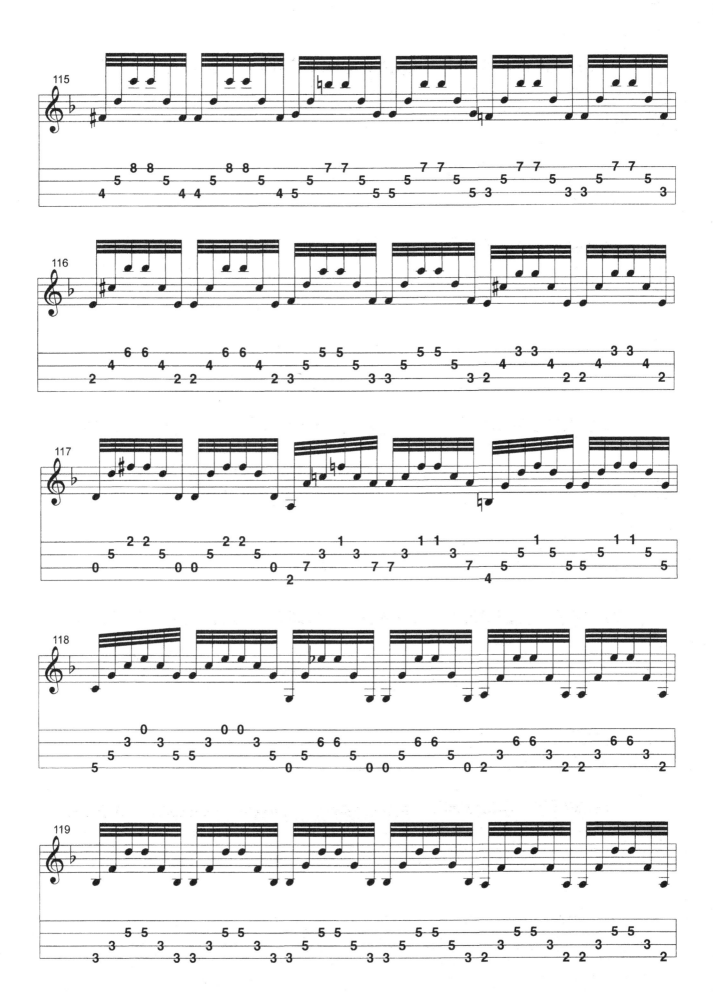

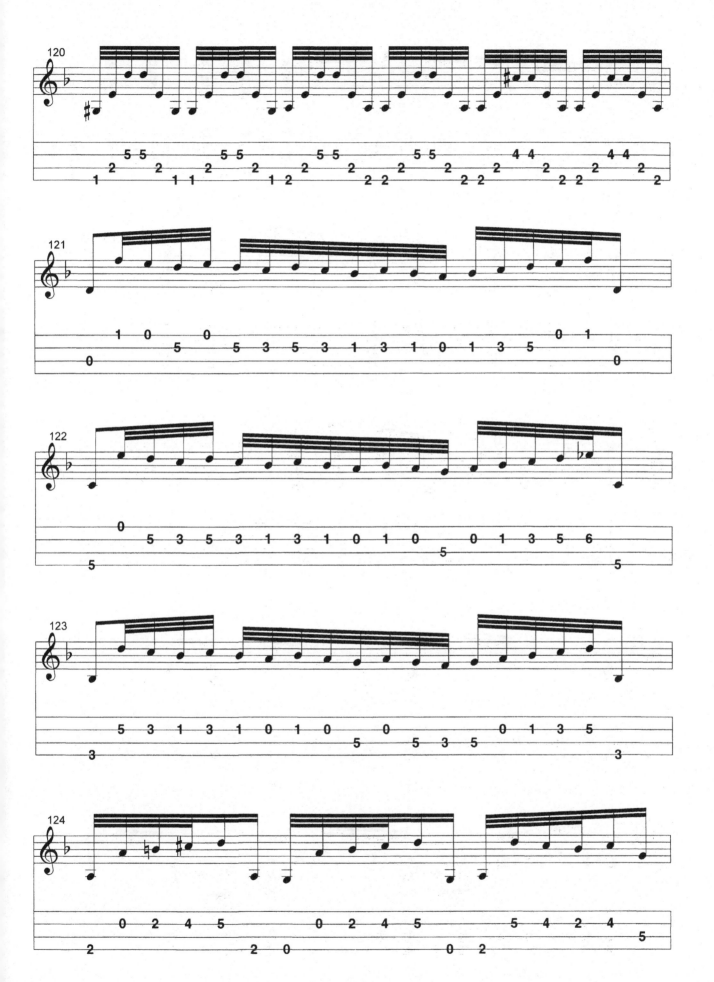

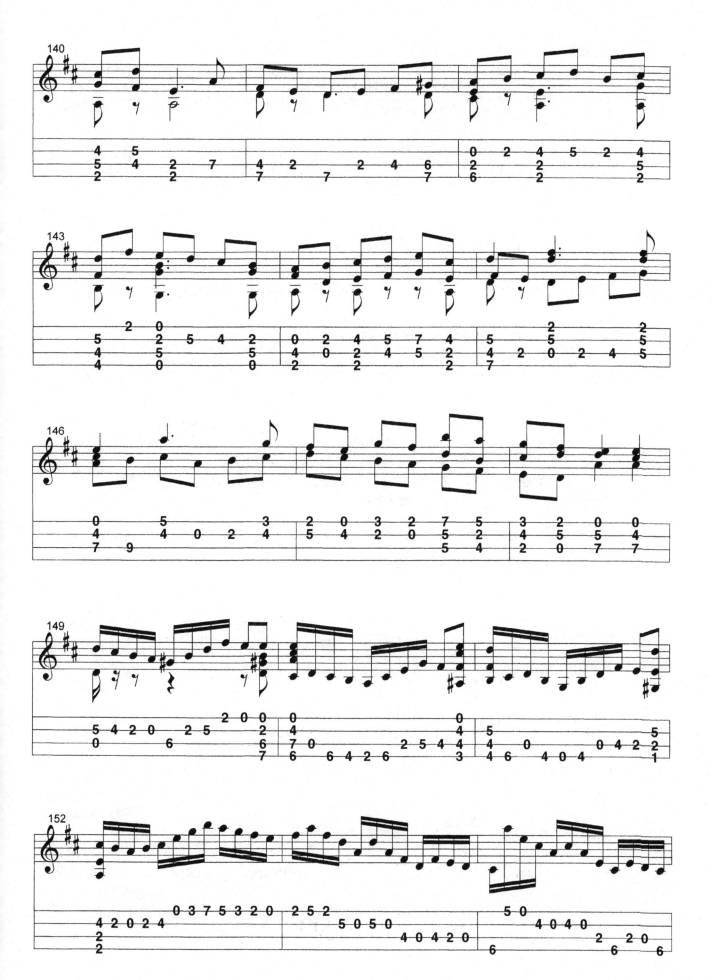

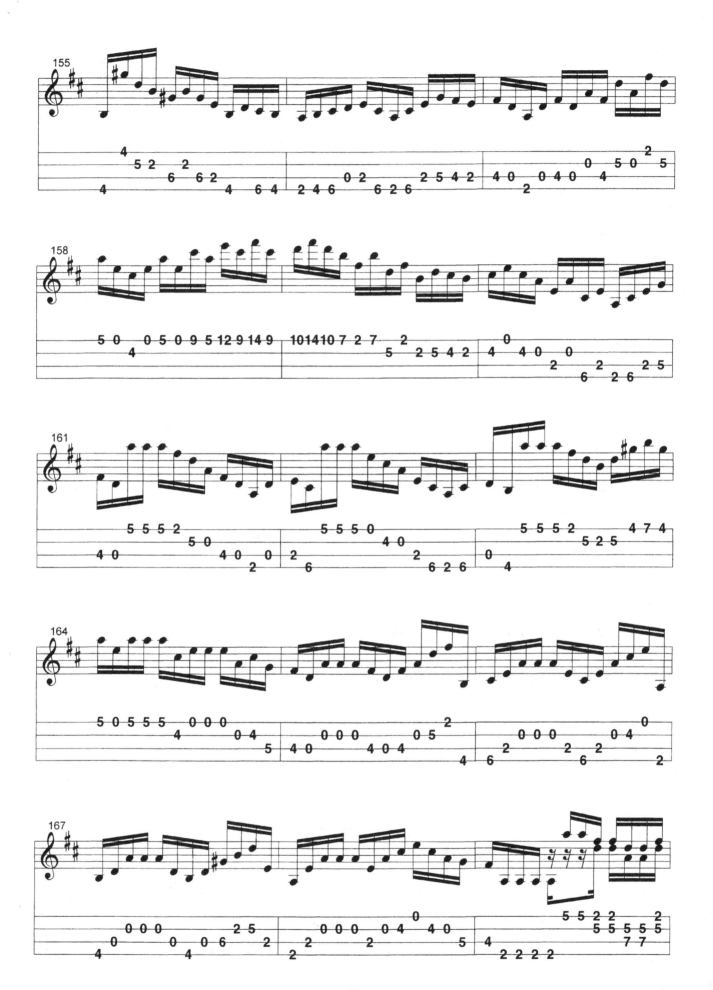

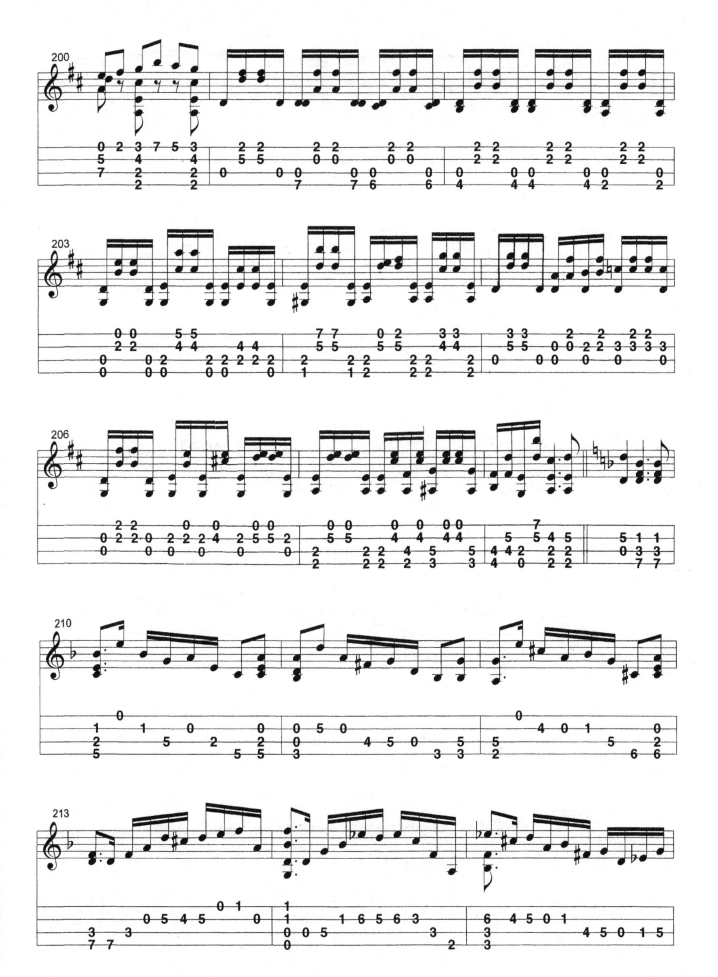

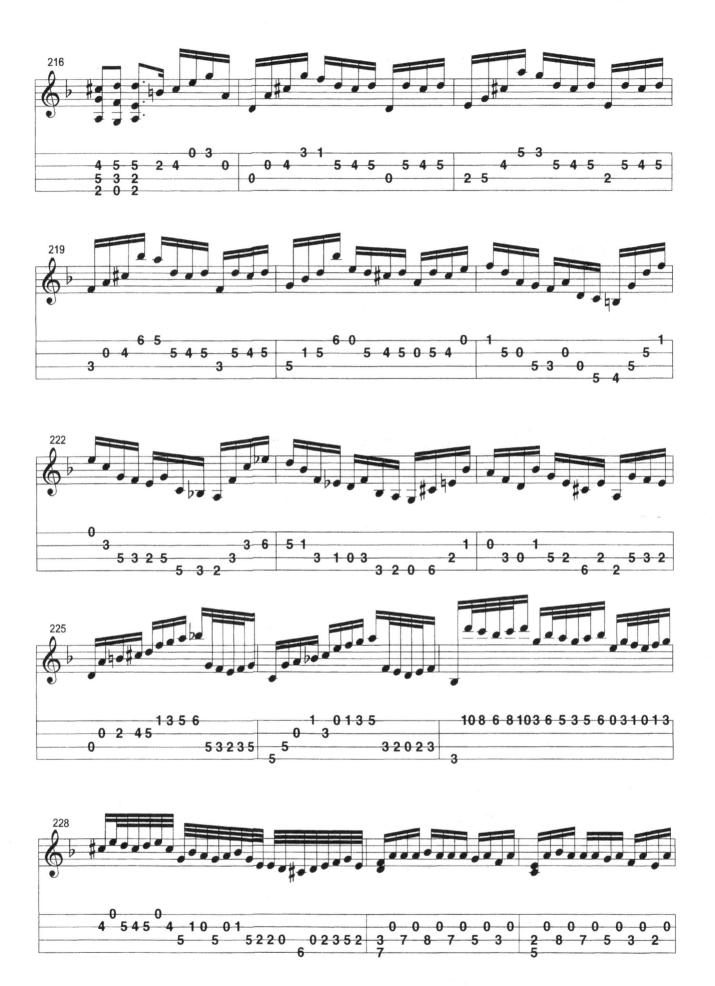

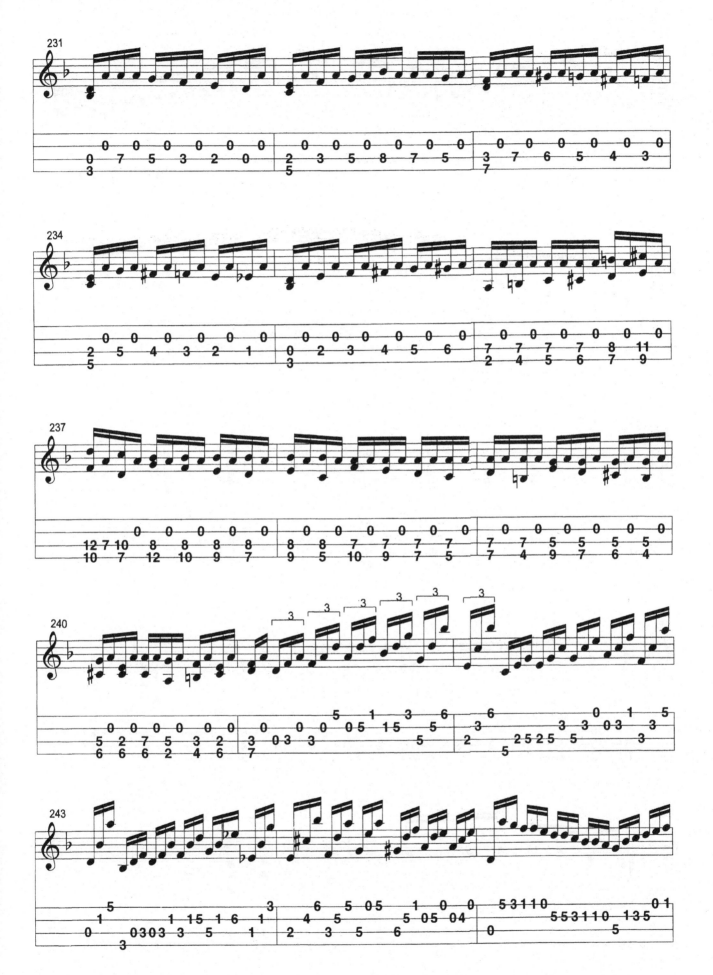

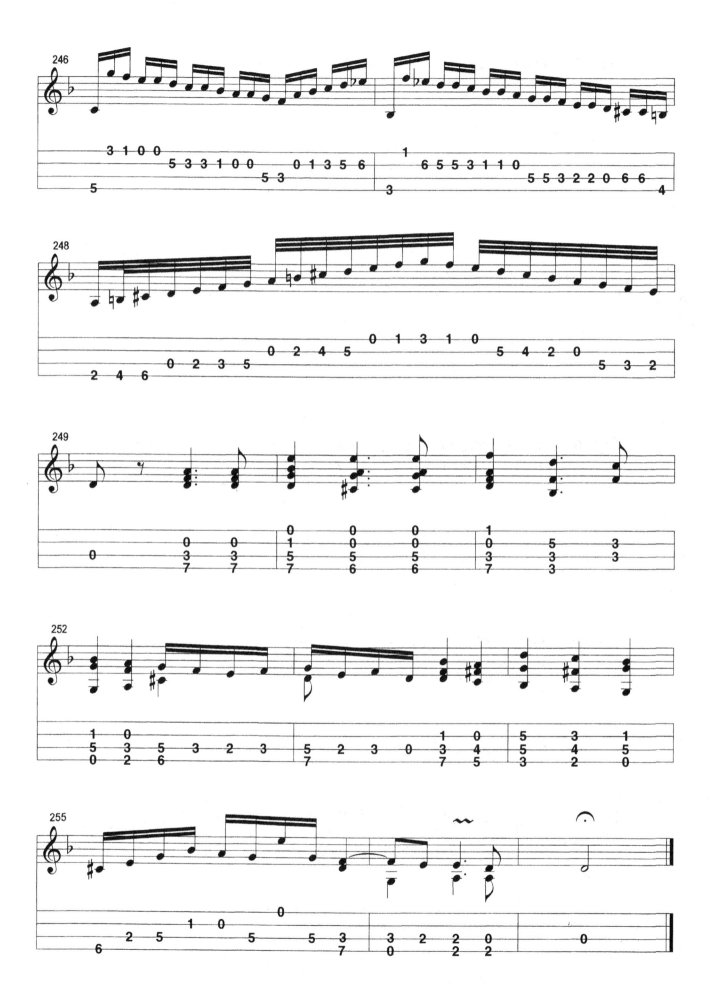

Bourrée

(from Orchestral Suite No. 3 in D)

Johann Sebastian Bach
(1685 - 1750)

Allegro

Menuet

(from Anna Magdalena Bach Book)

Johann Sebastian Bach
(1685 - 1750)

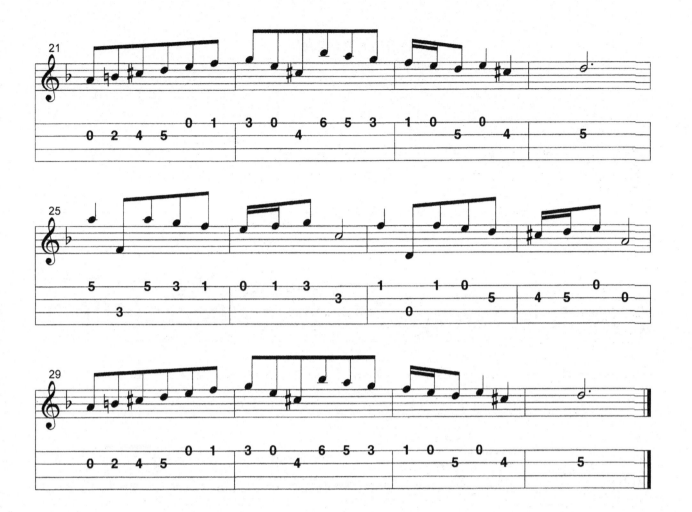

Sarabande

(from Orchestral Suite No. 2 in B minor)

Johann Sebastian Bach
(1685 - 1750)

Bourrée I
(from Orchestral Suite No. 2 in B minor)

Johann Sebastian Bach
(1685 - 1750)

Bourrée II
(from Orchestral Suite No. 2 in B minor)

Johann Sebastian Bach
(1685 - 1750)

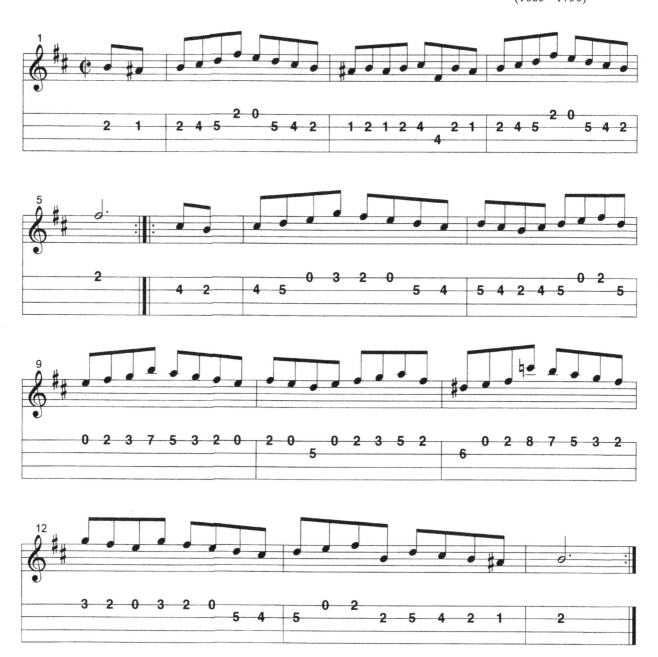

Bourrée I da Capo

Giga

(from Sonata # VI in E for solo violin)

Johann Sebastian Bach
(1685 - 1750)

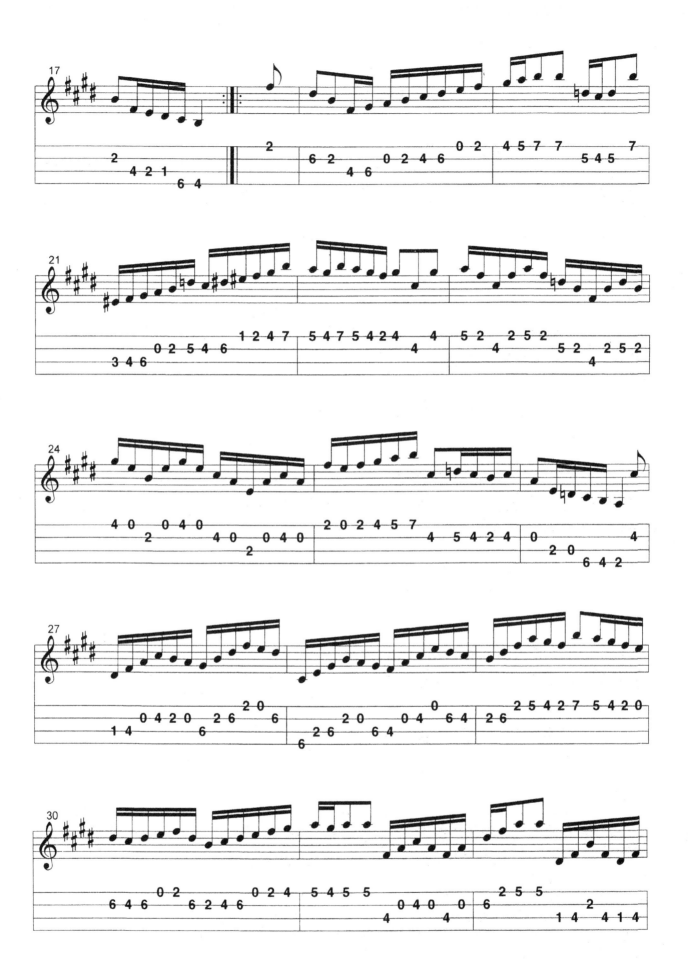

Violin Concerto No. I in A minor

(1st Movement)

Johann Sebastian Bach
(1685 - 1750)

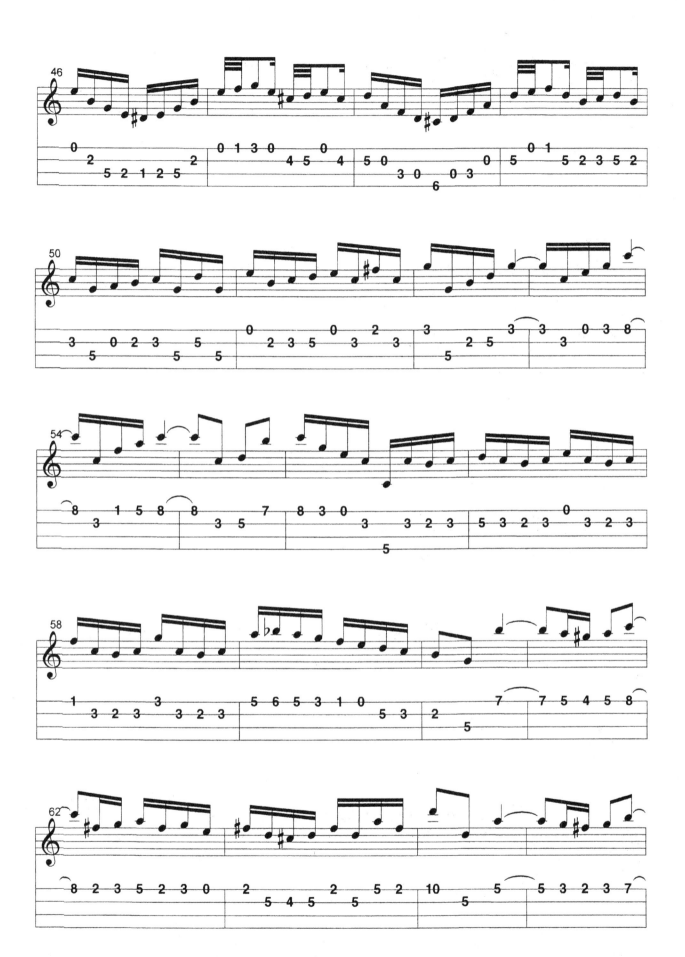

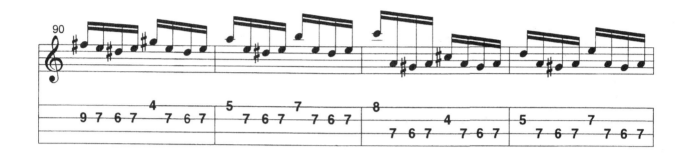

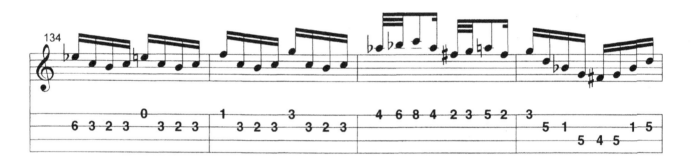

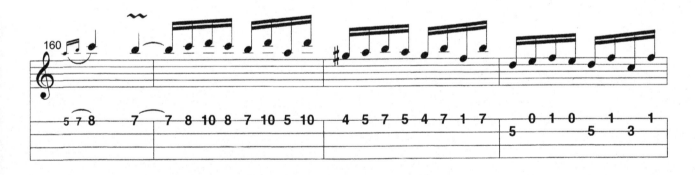

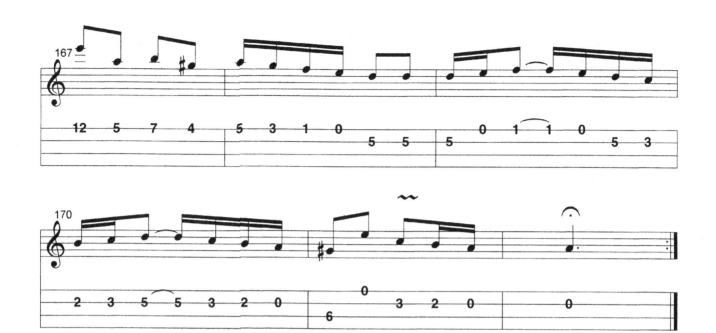

Sarabanda

(from Sonata No. 4 in D minor for solo Violin)

Johann Sebastian Bach
(1685 - 1750)

Made in the USA
Middletown, DE
21 September 2021